BASILOSAURUS

BY KATE MOENING
ILLUSTRATIONS BY MAT EDWARDS

EPIC

BELLWETHER MEDIA • MINNEAPOLIS, MN

EPIC

EPIC BOOKS are no ordinary books. They burst with intense action, high-speed heroics, and shadows of the unknown. Are you ready for an Epic adventure?

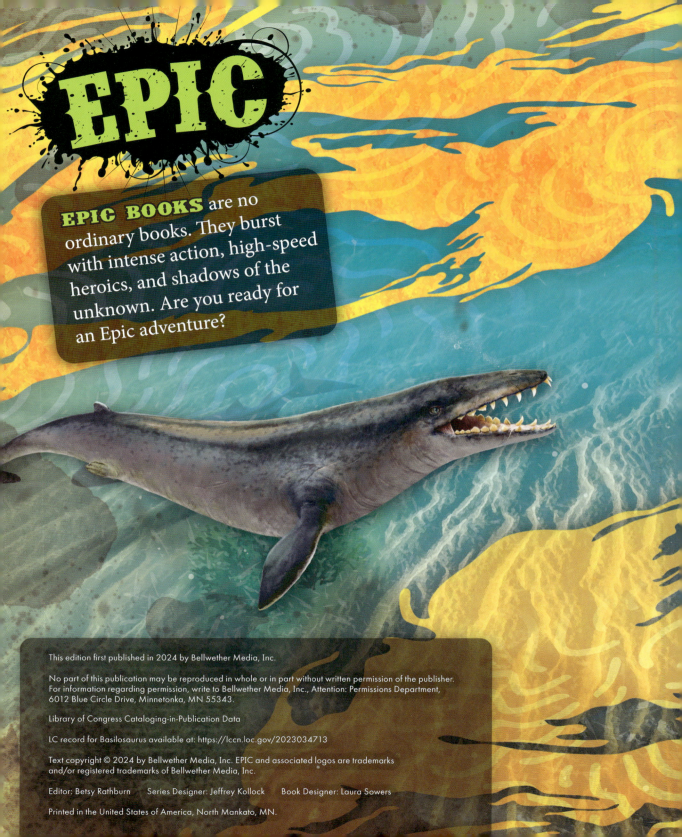

This edition first published in 2024 by Bellwether Media, Inc.

No part of this publication may be reproduced in whole or in part without written permission of the publisher. For information regarding permission, write to Bellwether Media, Inc., Attention: Permissions Department, 6012 Blue Circle Drive, Minnetonka, MN 55343.

Library of Congress Cataloging-in-Publication Data

LC record for Basilosaurus available at: https://lccn.loc.gov/2023034713

Text copyright © 2024 by Bellwether Media, Inc. EPIC and associated logos are trademarks and/or registered trademarks of Bellwether Media, Inc.

Editor: Betsy Rathburn   Series Designer: Jeffrey Kollock   Book Designer: Laura Sowers

Printed in the United States of America, North Mankato, MN.

TABLE OF CONTENTS

WHAT WAS THE BASILOSAURUS?	4
THE LIFE OF THE BASILOSAURUS	10
FOSSILS AND EXTINCTION	16
GET TO KNOW THE BASILOSAURUS	20
GLOSSARY	22
TO LEARN MORE	23
INDEX	24

WHAT WAS THE BASILOSAURUS?

PRONUNCIATION

BAS-ih-low-SORE-us

WHALE, ACTUALLY

Basilosaurus means "king lizard." Scientists thought the basilosaurus was a giant lizard at first!

MAP OF THE WORLD

Paleogene period

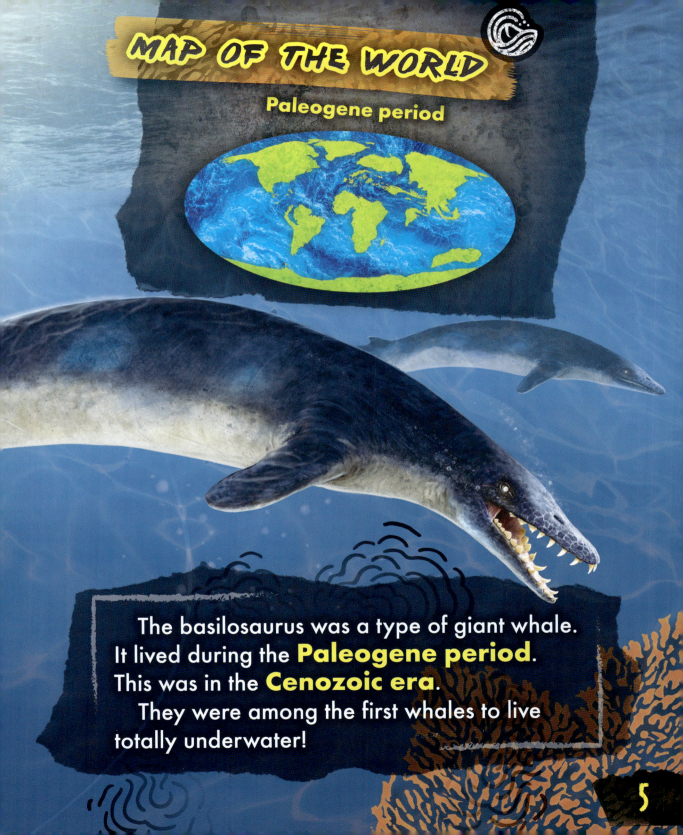

The basilosaurus was a type of giant whale. It lived during the **Paleogene period**. This was in the **Cenozoic era**.

They were among the first whales to live totally underwater!

Basilosaurus **ancestors** lived on land. They had strong back legs.

back leg

As the basilosaurus **evolved**, its legs got smaller. They were not strong enough to walk on land. The basilosaurus stayed in water!

The basilosaurus grew up to around 60 feet (18.3 meters) long. Its tail made up over half of its body length.
It used its tail to **propel** itself through the water. It used its front **flippers** to steer.

tail

flipper

SIZE COMPARISON

about as long as two school buses

9

THE LIFE OF THE BASILOSAURUS

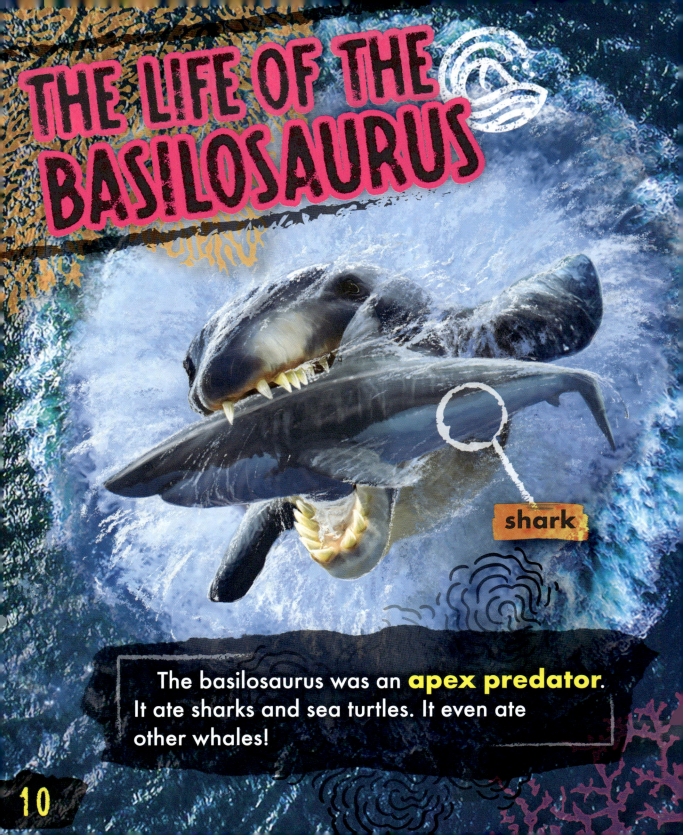

shark

The basilosaurus was an **apex predator**. It ate sharks and sea turtles. It even ate other whales!

The basilosaurus listened for **prey** underwater. It swam toward sounds to catch meals.

BASILOSAURUS DIET

sharks

sea turtles

whales

The basilosaurus had sharp, triangle-shaped teeth. It caught prey with its front teeth.

Then it tossed the prey into the back of its mouth. Its back teeth cut through tough pieces.

WHAT STRONG JAWS!

The basilosaurus was a powerful hunter. Its bite had 3,600 pounds (1,633 kilograms) of force. It could crush bones!

The basilosaurus stayed close to the ocean's surface. It was not able to dive deep.

This **mammal** gave birth to live young. Adults likely lived alone.

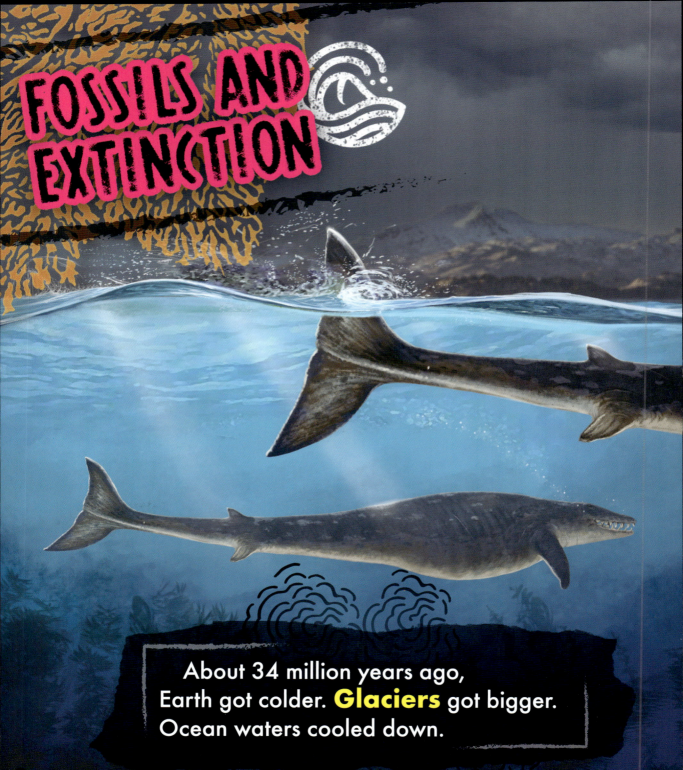

FOSSILS AND EXTINCTION

About 34 million years ago, Earth got colder. **Glaciers** got bigger. Ocean waters cooled down.

Many ocean animals could not survive these changes. The basilosaurus went **extinct**.

The first basilosaurus **fossils** were found in the southern United States. This was in the early 1830s.

Since then, many basilosaurus fossils have been found. Most were dug up in the southern U.S. and northern Africa.

WHALE VALLEY

Many whale fossils have been found at a park in Egypt. This used to be an ancient sea. People call the park Whale Valley!

fossil

FIRST BASILOSAURUS LEG FOSSIL

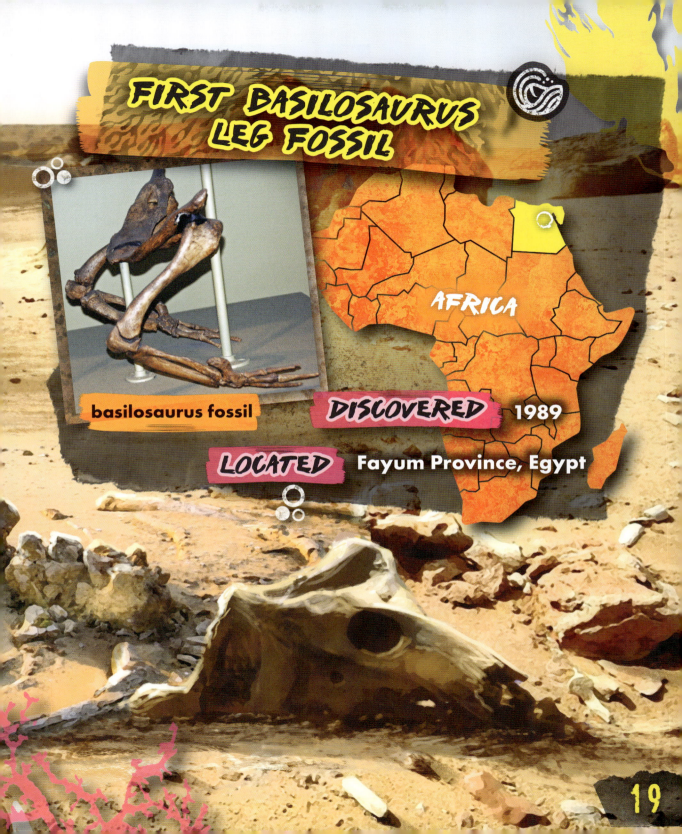

basilosaurus fossil

AFRICA

DISCOVERED 1989

LOCATED Fayum Province, Egypt

19

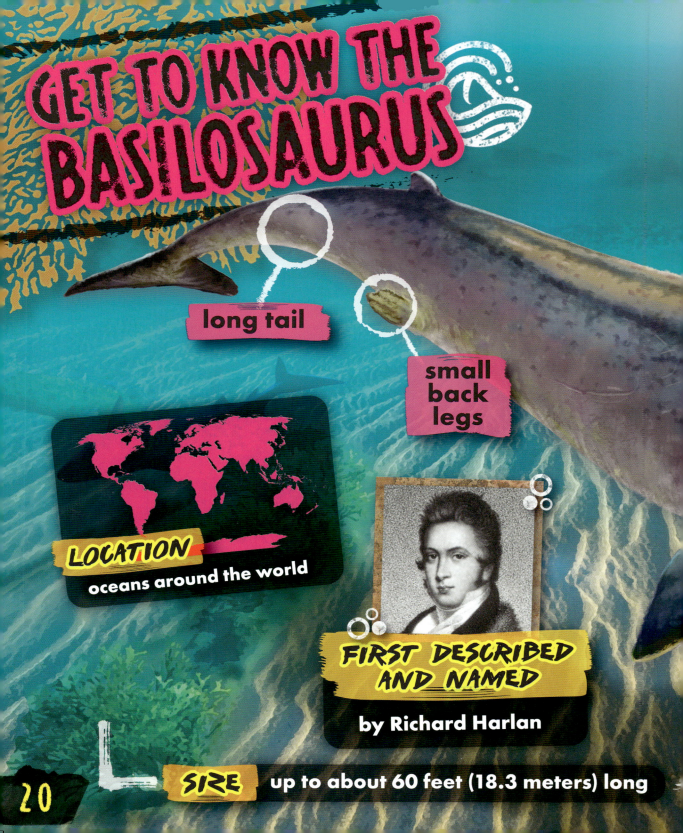

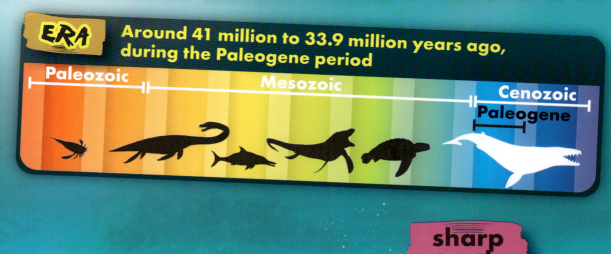

ERA Around 41 million to 33.9 million years ago, during the Paleogene period

Paleozoic | Mesozoic | Cenozoic | Paleogene

sharp teeth

front flippers

WEIGHT
up to 14,000 pounds
(6,350 kilograms)

FOOD
sharks
sea turtles
whales

21

GLOSSARY

ancestors—relatives that lived long ago

apex predator—an animal at the top of the food chain that is not preyed upon by other animals

Cenozoic era—a time in history that started 66 million years ago and continues to the present day

evolved—changed slowly over time

extinct—no longer living

flippers—flat body parts that are used for swimming

fossils—remains of a living thing that lived long ago

glaciers—massive sheets of ice that cover large areas of land

mammal—a warm-blooded animal that has a backbone and feeds its young milk

Paleogene period—the first period of the Cenozoic era; the Paleogene period lasted from about 66 million to 23 million years ago.

prey—animals that are hunted by other animals for food

propel—to push forward

To Learn More

AT THE LIBRARY

Dixon, Douglas. *When the Whales Walked and Other Incredible Evolutionary Journeys.* London, U.K.: Words & Pictures, 2018.

Moening, Kate. *Livyatan.* Minneapolis, Minn.: Bellwether Media, 2024.

Taylor, Charlotte. *Digging Up Sea Creature Fossils.* New York, N.Y.: Enslow Publishing, 2022.

ON THE WEB

Factsurfer.com gives you a safe, fun way to find more information.

1. Go to www.factsurfer.com.

2. Enter "basilosaurus" into the search box and click 🔍.

3. Select your book cover to see a list of related content.

INDEX

Africa, 18
ancestors, 6
apex predator, 10
back legs, 6, 7
bite, 13
Cenozoic era, 5
Egypt, 18
evolved, 7
extinct, 17
flippers, 8, 9
food, 10, 11, 12
fossils, 18, 19
get to know, 20–21
glaciers, 16
land, 6, 7

mammal, 15
map, 5, 19
name, 4
ocean, 14, 16, 17
Paleogene period, 5
prey, 10, 11, 12
pronunciation, 4
scientists, 4
size, 8, 9
tail, 8
teeth, 12
United States, 18
water, 5, 7, 8, 11, 16
whale, 5, 10, 18
young, 15

The images in this book are reproduced through the courtesy of: Mat Edwards, front cover, pp. 1, 2-3, 4-5, 6-7, 8-9, 10-11, 12-13, 14-15, 16-17, 18-19, 20-21; James St. John, p. 19 (fossil); Michele Pekenino/ Wikipedia, p. 20 (Richard Harlan).